W0010330

One-Minute
PRAYERS®
for
Young Women

Hope Lyda

HARVEST HOUSE PUBLISHERS
EUGENE, OREGON

Cover design by Bryce Williamson

Cover photo © aunaauna / Getty Images

ONE-MINUTE PRAYERS is a registered trademark of The Hawkins Children's LLC. Harvest House Publishers, Inc., is the exclusive licensee of the federally registered trademark ONE-MINUTE PRAYERS.

One-Minute Prayers® for Young Women Deluxe Edition
Copyright © 2012 by Hope Lyda
Published by Harvest House Publishers
Eugene, Oregon 97408
www.harvesthousepublishers.com

ISBN 978-0-7369-8051-7 (Milano Softone™)
ISBN 978-0-7369-4984-2 (eBook)

Printed in China

20 21 22 23 24 25 26 27 / RDS-CD / 10 9 8 7 6 5 4 3 2 1

To Anna Gossard Schultz,
an amazing young woman.
In loving memory of Paul Gossard—
her father and this book's gracious editor.

Contents

HEART TO HEART
ABOUT GOD

God is a true friend. Now, it might sound a little far-fetched to say, "Jesus is my best friend," but when you face life's difficulties and deep joys, you begin to understand how true this statement is. Your Lord—and the maker of your heart and mind, with all their complexities—is a generous, loving, forgiving, and *personal* God.

As you discover more about who God is and what He's like, as well as discovering these things about yourself, you'll be inspired to follow His lead a bit more each day… each month…each year. God's loyalty and consistency offer you a foundation of security…and that security will help you give and be your very best.

Your relationship with God will be strengthened the more you talk to Him through prayer. If it doesn't feel "normal" to talk to God yet, give it time, and give Him time as He's at work in your heart and life. When you aren't even sure what to say or what to ask, God is in the middle of the silence. He'll know what your heart needs.

Prayer Starter:

God, I need You for many things. And since You created my life, You know just what I need and when I need it. Sometimes it feels like You are far away and not involved in my life. I believe that You are near and that You care. Help my beliefs and my feelings line up as I spend more time talking to You. I really want to feel that You are my Lord and friend.

Right now, I need to feel that You're with me as I face these situations:

-
-
-

I'm grateful for Your friendship, God. As I learn how to talk to You and how to trust the times of silence and of waiting, I know that You are with me and that You are making me into the young woman I am meant to become. Amen.

Prayer

PRAYERS RISING

May my prayer be set before you like incense;
may the lifting up of my hands be like the evening sacrifice.

Psalm 141:2

God, I'm still discovering how to talk to You. Sometimes
it's easy, because in a difficult moment I call out for help.
But when I'm not in a mini-crisis, I don't know what to
say. I hate to admit it, but I've had times of doubt about
whether my prayers matter. Yet I know You're here with me.
I like to imagine my prayers rising up to Your heart like
smoke rising from a campfire. While the warmth comforts me and Your light brightens my outlook, my words
gently spiral their way to Your accepting ears. You don't
rush me, and You never think what I have to say is insignificant. I can't wait to talk to You more often, Lord.

CALLING GOD

Because he turned his ear to me,
I will call on him as long as I live.

PSALM 116:2

You gave me Your personal number and You are available anytime to take my calls. That's the miracle of prayer. I can call to You, and You turn an ear to me and listen. You don't tell me to try back at a more convenient time. You don't say, "Hold on" and then finish playing a computer game or start a conversation with someone else while I wait.

God, Your attentive ear shows me how attentive You are to my heart. As I go about my day, I talk to You and ask for Your input and guidance, and for reminders of Your promises. Let me also be a good listener as I wait for Your answers for me. And may my first call to You always be with words of gratitude.

MAKING A NEW HABIT

Be joyful in hope, patient in affliction, faithful in prayer.
Share with the Lord's people who are
in need. Practice hospitality.

ROMANS 12:12-13

I'm grateful for the hope You bring to my life, Lord. I'm eager for the practice of prayer to become a regular part of my life. When I am experiencing happy moments with friends or laughing with my family, may I thank You for the gift of joy. When I face a school day that overflows with mini-disasters or mistakes, may I patiently await the comfort of Your peace and the refreshment of Your generous heart.

As prayer becomes second nature for me, I hope that I can encourage others. I want to see their needs and hopes so I can be compassionate. Show me how to do these things, Lord, and help me want to come to You for everything.

PRAYER POWER

The prayer offered in faith will make the sick person well;
the Lord will raise them up. If they have sinned, they
will be forgiven. Therefore confess your sins to each other
and pray for each other so that you may be healed. The
prayer of a righteous person is powerful and effective.

JAMES 5:15-16

Lord, I come to You today with the broken parts of me lifted up for Your care. I have hurts that need Your healing, and sins that require the mending of Your forgiveness. I'm realizing that prayer isn't just about asking for things—it's about bringing the pieces of my life to You so I can see Your power to make me whole.

Sometimes I pretend to be okay so that I don't have to deal with friends asking me what is wrong, but I want to be vulnerable to You—open with You always. Each time I ask for Your help to overcome my heartaches and flaws, I experience the incredible feeling of being known and loved unconditionally.

Plans

TODAY MATTERS

Whatever your hand finds to do, do it with all your might.

ECCLESIASTES 9:10

Today *is* the first day of the rest of my life. Even though that sounds like a hyped-up motivational poster, it actually makes me happy! I believe You give me this day to make a difference, God. This moment is a new beginning. It is a chance to give 150 percent to all that I do. I have lazy days when I want to crawl back under the covers and forget about any plans that have been made. But today, I'm eager to see what You have in store for me. I pray that my words, actions, prayers, and decisions make a difference.

Give me a strong sense of Your guidance so that my efforts and commitment would play a part in turning an ordinary day into an extraordinary example of living life completely for You.

CHANGE OF PLANS

*There is no wisdom, no insight, no plan
that can succeed against the Lord.*

Proverbs 21:30

God, I have so many things to do and so many plans in the making. I've shown You my lists! And You've heard my prayers packed with ideas and intentions. I'm giving so much attention to *my* plans that I have forgotten to ask about Your plans for me and my faith journey. I'm still learning how to depend on You for direction, but I want You to guide my steps, Lord.

I know that when I walk in Your way, I'll still encounter rough spots, but I'll be able to face them with greater peace and trust. As I change my plans and to-do lists to line up with Your will, may I seek Your guidance, Your priorities, and Your strength.

YOU INCLUDE ME

The plans of the Lord stand firm forever,
the purposes of his heart through all generations.

Psalm 33:11

I like being a part of Your legacy, Lord. The work You do in and through me is a way I have a role in Your big picture. When I feel insignificant around someone who seems on top of the world, I will rest in the truth that I am part of Your plan for today and tomorrow. If I second-guess my abilities, I will be reminded to give my circumstances over to Your strength and ability.

I don't know what tomorrow will look like. Some of my dreams will come true, and some of them will fade away. But Your plans are forever. And today, like every day, You invite me to be a part of Your purpose and compassion for the world. Thanks for including me! I love You, God.

SET ME ON COURSE

In their hearts humans plan their course,
but the LORD establishes their steps.

PROVERBS 16:9

Lord, You know my heart has held many dreams and expectations over the years. But lately, I'm not so sure what I want or even what step to take next. I'm just gazing into the distance without a focus. My moods often alter how I respond to situations and how I make decisions! I want to be entrusting each step to Your plan and not to my uncertain whims.

God, set me on the right course. Guide me to embrace priorities and plans that match up with Yours. Things change. Sometimes so quickly, I lose my footing. But as I turn to face Your course with renewed commitment, I know You won't let me fall.

Grace

WHO I AM

Do not think of yourself more highly than you ought, but rather think of yourself with sober judgment, in accordance with the faith God has distributed to each of you.

ROMANS 12:3

I love to experience success. It boosts my confidence in all that I do for a while. But I know that when I shine the light on my own effort as the reason for that success, then I've missed out on a chance to rely on what You want to give me. I'm devaluing my relationship with You when I take all the credit for my talents, my perseverance during hard times, and my opportunities.

Thank You for my faith. I don't think about that much, but the truth is that I'm incredibly grateful for my relationship with You. When I take leaps of faith, I jump into Your arms and say, "Catch me!" And You always do, Lord. Remind me to give the glory to You for every evidence of Your faithfulness.

WHEREVER I GO

*The grace of the Lord Jesus Christ
be with your spirit. Amen.*

PHILIPPIANS 4:23

I never thought about it before, but Your grace goes with me wherever I go. It isn't just experienced at church or when I'm praying in my room. You fill my spirit with Your forgiveness and mercy so that I can take it into the world. I have Your grace in my heart because You are in my heart.

I'm devoting my decisions and actions to You today, Lord. I want to reflect Your gift of grace through my words and deeds. May I develop a heart of compassion that does not hesitate to extend grace to others, including the student in class who frustrates me, the teacher who doesn't get me, my family when they start to bother me, my friend who lets me down. I pray for those people I encounter throughout the day…may they come to know Your mercy.

THE LANGUAGE OF GRACE

*Let your conversation be always full
of grace, seasoned with salt,
so that you may know how to answer everyone.*

COLOSSIANS 4:6

Tongue-tied! It happens to me all the time, Lord. When I try to share about my faith with a friend or someone new in my life and I get flustered or nervous. When I talk about making it through difficult times of stress, anger, or pain, and I don't always reveal that You're my source of comfort.

Give me the right words at the right time so I can express myself in ways that honor You. I want my friends to know You like I am starting to know You. Teach me the language of grace so that I'm always willing and able to offer a word of kindness, hope, and encouragement.

REMEMBER ME

Do not remember the sins of my youth
and my rebellious ways;
according to your love remember me,
for you, Lord, are good.

PSALM 25:7

How often have I heard Your direction to release my past sins to You? And I've even been encouraged by teachers and leaders to rest in Your forgiveness. But I still hold onto my past mistakes. In fact, I dwell on them. They haunt me because they've impacted me and others, and because I've let You down.

I am ready to let go of my mistakes and hold on to Your love, which is so much bigger than my errors. The baggage of my sins is no more. You've cast them from Your memory. You saved me from them long ago. And You accept me as Your child living in Your all-goodness. Thank You, Lord, for releasing hold of my sin and for never, ever letting go of me.

Friendship

A FAITHFUL FRIEND

My intercessor is my friend
as my eyes pour out tears to God;
on behalf of a man he pleads with God
as one pleads for a friend.

JOB 16:20-21

God, I long to have a friend who is prayerful. It would be so wonderful to know that someone cares this much about me. Thank You for those people in my life who have thought to lift me up to Your heart over the years. Let me be encouraged by the prayers spoken on my behalf by known and unknown prayer warriors around me.

Just as I love the idea of someone praying for me regularly, Lord, I also love the idea of being a faithful, praying friend for others. Give me the desire and urgency to pray for friends with devotion. I want to develop my spiritual attention so that I am more aware of what to bring to You in prayer for those who make up my world.

GOD FRIENDS

I am a friend to all who fear you,
to all who follow your precepts.

Psalm 119:63

Lord, thank You for bringing people of faith into my life. My path is not always straight. I wander. I take detours that easily make me forget the path You set me on just months, weeks, or days before. I'm very grateful for the friends and family who guide me back to Your way. By staying true to Your truths, these people are supporting me and my unique purpose as a young woman of faith.

When I meet someone new and discover that they are a person of faith, I have a strong sense of connection with them right away. It is such an encouragement to me when I see someone at school following Your will. Give me boldness to be open about my faith so others will feel at ease to share about their own beliefs or their doubts. I wouldn't know You like I do if others had kept quiet about their convictions. Help me to become a friend who cares enough to share about the most important relationship a girl can ever have.

KNOWING YOU

Anyone who chooses to be a friend of the
world becomes an enemy of God.

JAMES 4:4

God, I don't consider myself a worldly person. I care about my friends and I'm committed to my faith. But I've been thinking lately about how easy it is, more often than not, to befriend the world. I focus on what I wear, how I look, what others think of me, what I think of others, and what I really want that I don't have. That's a lot of time invested in the world.

Help me develop a deeper friendship with You. I want to know You better, and I want my heart to be in line with Your hopes and purposes for me. As I draw closer to You, I know the other things will matter less and less. And the best part is, my relationship with You will show me how to be a generous, faithful friend to others.

TRUE FRIEND

*Two are better than one, because they have a good
return for their labor: if either of them falls down,
one can help the other up. But pity anyone
who falls and has no one to help them up.*

ECCLESIASTES 4:9-10

Lord, I want to find a true friend of the heart. There are people I connect with, laugh with, and talk to—yet I still feel a bit lonely sometimes. I want to know that there is someone who has my back in life and who prays for me and wants the best for me. I'd like to believe there is another girl who would love to talk about faith and doubt and what it is like to maneuver through life as a teen.

Please let me be open to who this friend might be. Perhaps it is someone already in my life. Maybe You are directing a stranger to cross paths with me. Keep me from being judgmental or too shy, so that I don't miss the opportunity to see someone for who they really are—a friend in the making. While I keep this hope in my heart, Lord, show me how to be a good and loving friend to my family members and to each person You bring into my life.

Becoming Me

WHAT'S NEXT?

The LORD will vindicate me;
your love, LORD, endures forever—
do not abandon the works of your hands.

PSALM 138:8

Will I ever feel as though I have arrived? I'm still waiting to stand on the solid ground of understanding what life is about. I know I'm still young, but I don't like being in the dark about my purpose and my gifts. I might like to read mysteries, but when it comes to my life, I want answers. Give me patience, Lord.

I truly believe that You have planted seeds of good things in my life. I'm only now discovering some of my interests and how they fit with my personality and my dreams. Lord, work out what You want in me and through me. Make my days fruitful. Guide me in my choices and in my attitude so I don't overlook the ways I'm becoming the person You created me to be.

SHOW ME THE WAY

In him we were also chosen, having been
predestined according to the
plan of him who works out everything in
conformity with the purpose of his will,
in order that we, who were the first to put our hope
in Christ, might be for the praise of his glory.

Ephesians 1:11-12

Show me the way to go, Lord. I have several decisions to make, and I want to know what the right choices are. My hope is in You to guide me and give me wisdom, even when I face uncertainty and weakness.

I'm Your daughter. I know You care about every step I take. You are working out Your will in my life. This comforts me because I find life confusing sometimes. Okay, a lot of the time. Because I have faith and I've seen how You do answer prayer, I'm able to believe wholeheartedly that difficult times are opportunities to lean on You all the more. Show me the way to my higher purpose today and tomorrow, and give me a heart that is ready and willing to follow.

SHOWING YOU TO OTHERS

*It does not...depend on human desire or effort,
but on God's mercy. For Scripture says to Pharaoh:
"I raised you up for this very purpose, that I
might display my power in you and that my
name might be proclaimed in all the earth."*

ROMANS 9:16-17

People don't always see the full me. They see who they
think I am. They don't realize that when I take on challenges or rise to the occasion, I'm doing it through You
and in Your power.

Only You can lift me up to a place of influence or
strength. May I tell everyone about what You've done in
my life. May Your great purposes be seen in my small
actions and achievements.

BENEATH IT ALL

Many are the plans in a person's heart,
but it is the LORD's purpose that prevails.

PROVERBS 19:21

Beneath my actions and my dreams, my hopes and my efforts, is a current of purpose set in motion by Your hand. Even though I try to hear Your heart, I am not always certain if my desires are of Your great plan for me. But day by day I give to You my devotion and my best intentions.

Please mold my human efforts into Your divine plan. Create in me sensitivity to how You lead me so that I serve a purpose bigger than my own.

ENCOURAGED

*My goal is that they may be encouraged in heart and
united in love, so that they may have the full riches of
complete understanding, in order that they may know
the mystery of God, namely, Christ, in whom are
hidden all the treasures of wisdom and knowledge.*

Colossians 2:2-3

When I'm discouraged, I take heart in the love You've
shown me in the past. I have seen Your mercy in the kindness of others, Your support in the gift of friendship, and
Your wisdom through godly teachers.

These glimpses of who You are and how You provide
for me are reminders that my life has meaning. Your
purpose not only shapes who I am becoming, but fills my
heart with eternal treasures.

HEART TO HEART
ABOUT FAITH

How does your faith in God affect your life and the way you live it? Do you think about Him during the day? Do you talk with your Creator when you face difficulties or reach important goals? Imagine how much the Creator of the universe could do through you if you opened up your life to more: more of His power. More of His goodness. More of His grace.

Being a Christian should impact your life in big ways. It's like receiving sight after being blind for a dozen years...all of a sudden you can see how you are a part of God's action in the world. Your uniqueness is an important piece of the universe's puzzle. Wouldn't it be sad to miss out on knowing this wonderful truth about yourself?

Pick a day this week that you'll think about how God is working through you at any and every moment of the day. Consider how God is acting through you and using your life and abilities to serve a bigger purpose. If you have a journal or a blog, maybe write about how your day went with this new perspective.

Was anything different? Did you view happenings or people differently? Did God feel more a part of your daily life? In what ways did you feel He was leading you? Did any of your friends notice a change?

Prayer Starter:

Thank You for creating me as me, Lord. In many ways, I'm just beginning to appreciate the life You have given me. Help me use it for good things. Direct my steps so I walk in Your ways. I want to discover all the wonderful aspects of life You are hoping to show me during my lifetime. Right now I pray about areas in my life that don't make sense:

-

-

-

Help me see Your hand on my life in these situations or circumstances. It feels good to be heard, God. I am lucky to know You. Amen.

Belief

WHEN I FIRST BELIEVED

We ought always to thank God for you, brothers and
sisters loved by the Lord, because from the beginning
God chose you to be saved through the sanctifying
work of the Spirit and through belief in the truth.

2 THESSALONIANS 2:13

When I first experienced a deep belief in Your everlasting love, I understood that You knew me, chose me, and were eager to lead me. I thank You for knowing how much I would need You, especially now. You knew then that I would experience the hurts and the difficulties I am facing now. And today You speak promises into my life that will unfold in my future.

Give me an authentic understanding of what it means to be a person of faith. Belief isn't the whole story...it was just the beginning of my great adventure with You. I'm excited to see how You will continue to transform me from the inside out.

YES, LORD

When he had gone indoors, the blind men
came to him, and he asked them, "Do you
believe that I am able to do this?"
"Yes, Lord," they replied.

MATTHEW 9:28

I'm so ready to put my faith into action. I've seen how You are at work in the lives of the people I respect most. And I know You've changed my heart from the first day I met You. Now, I feel more prepared to say "Yes" and more willing to give over each day's joys, troubles, conflicts, and decisions to Your power.

I'm so lucky that I see You as the Lord of my life. You offer healing, second chances, unconditional love, and the boundless joy of acceptance. Yes, Lord…I believe You are able to do great things in my life.

LOOKING FOR A PLACE TO LAND

If any of you lacks wisdom, you should ask God, who gives generously to all without finding fault, and it will be given to you. But when you ask, you must believe and not doubt, because the one who doubts is like a wave of the sea, blown and tossed by the wind.

JAMES 1:5-6

I've watched kites bounce around on a windy day. I've seen baby ducks bobbing up and down as the lake ripples and swells. There are times that I'm caught in the wind and water currents myself. Pulled down, thrown here, tossed there, and pushed aside as I fight to keep my momentum going the right direction: Your direction. It's not easy, God. There are many forces and undercurrents that rise up behind me and beneath me. They take me by surprise, and when I end up far from where I want to be, I call out to You, yet again, to bring me back to the path You have for my life.

Lord, I pray for the strength of faith to endure the doubts and the trials so that I can always remain on a course set by Your truths and land firmly in the place Your heart wants me.

IS IT ENOUGH?

Jesus turned and saw her. "Take heart, daughter,"
he said, "your faith has healed you." And the
woman was healed at that moment.

MATTHEW 9:22

I think of the woman in this verse whom You healed. You
called her "daughter" and said her faith had healed her.
Do I have that kind of faith, Lord? I know that You hear
the pain of my heart and mend the broken places of my
spirit. But when I'm lost and stuck in a difficult situation,
will I follow my faith and reach out to You?

Lord, I give my daily steps to You to lead me. I pray
that when I stumble, my first impulse will be to touch the
hem of Your grace. And in the moments when it is difficult for me to see beyond my circumstances, please give
me the belief I need. I long to hear You call me "daughter."

I KNOW YOU HEAR ME

LORD, I wait for you;
you will answer, LORD my God.

PSALM 38:15

Lord—I have called out to You, and I'm trying to be patient as I wait for Your help. I'm so empty right now. My friends and family try to encourage me with words, but I can't seem to absorb those good intentions. I need the comfort of Your love. You know me so well. You see the places of my heart and my life that I hold back from the world. I place my faith in You. I know You hear me and will answer my cries for comfort.

When I speak to You in the quiet of the night, I feel the worry leave me. It is replaced with peace, and I know that I have been heard—You are here with me.

Generosity

OPEN ARMS

She opens her arms to the poor
and extends her hands to the needy.

Proverbs 31:20

Who needs my help today? I want to ask this question so that I become more aware of the opportunities that exist all around me to serve others. I can make sure to invite other girls into a conversation my friends are having. When we choose groups for projects, I can include someone I don't know well. God, give me courage to spark a conversation with someone who seems shy, hurt, or lonely.

My actions to assist another one of Your children become a part of Your will for that person. You are not calling me to fix them or to make all their trouble go away—after all, only You can do that. My job is to open my heart and my arms to others.

LET THE BLESSINGS FLOW

*You will be enriched in every way so that
you can be generous on every occasion,
and through us your generosity will
result in thanksgiving to God.*

2 Corinthians 9:11

I'm rich! Okay, I never thought I'd say that. But the more time I spend with You, the more I recognize my blessings and opportunities as wealth. Lord, help me freely give what I do have, including material possessions and spiritual strength. When I'm tempted to withhold my time, my belongings, or my compassion, it's because I'm afraid I'll lose control of my cozy world.

Connect me with the people who need what I can provide. Expand my heart so that I make room for generosity and hospitality. My obedience can turn another person's cry for help into songs of thanksgiving. Don't let me miss out on the chance to multiply my riches by sharing them again and again.

READY FOR REFRESHMENT

A generous person will prosper;
whoever refreshes others will be refreshed.

PROVERBS 11:25

Family, health, opportunity, faith, shelter, friends. These gifts from You are my foundation and support. I feel You leading me to share them, so I'm brainstorming how to do this. I can invite a friend to have dinner with my family. I can encourage someone I don't see often with a handwritten note or an e-mail. I can even use my health by participating in a fund-raiser walk or helping an elderly neighbor with chores. There are many ways for me to extend what You give me to others.

As soon as I help someone, I am refreshed and energized. And I always feel Your deep joy when I follow through. Fill me with the delight of giving. And may my offerings refresh the spirit of another.

WHAT GIFTS DO I BRING?

*If anyone serves, they should do so with the
strength God provides, so that in all things God
may be praised through Jesus Christ. To him be
the glory and the power for ever and ever.*

1 Peter 4:11

I am always moved by the Christmas song "The Little
Drummer Boy." When I tell myself that I have nothing
of value to offer You or the people in my life, I think of
the poor boy with no tangible gifts to give his newborn
Savior. He realizes he has himself and a song on his drum
to offer, so he gives his all.

Offering what I have is the simple solution—yet I
rarely feel like what I have or what I am is good enough
or even wanted. That's the negative self-talk taking over.
You made me. You love me. The confidence I receive from
these truths leads me to give my all to You by giving to
others through prayer, obedience, faith, and forgiveness.

DOING GOOD

Who is going to harm you if you are eager to do good?

1 PETER 3:13

I want to change the world. I believe that a lot of people in my generation are becoming aware of ways to make a difference. I love that we can impact others when we follow up good and godly ideas with action. One moment of giving can turn a bad situation into a blessing. The power to change lives and hearts is activated when I act on the impulse to serve You.

Lord, my heart is eager. Direct it to do good so that I serve Your purpose, which is higher, and not my own. You smile upon a child who desires to please You. Your love embraces me and holds me close in the security of Your mercy. How can I not be excited to share this comfort with others? I hope You are proud of Your girl.

Truth

YOUR WAY

I have chosen the way of faithfulness;
I have set my heart on your laws.

Psalm 119:30

I'm so thankful I discovered the truth of Your love when I did. I was all over the place seeking answers to random questions. I didn't know what to ask in my quest for understanding and identity. But You showed me that I could entrust my heart and future to You. It felt so good to be embraced by Your acceptance as I embraced the truth of Your love.

I still have times of confusion and questions. I still have obstacles to overcome, and I have a lot of growing to do as a young woman of faith. But now I am never without a measure of truth to guide me. Now my many questions are replaced by one request: "Show me the way, Lord."

REALITY ME

We know…that the Son of God has come
and has given us understanding,
so that we may know him who is true.
And we are in him who is true
by being in his Son Jesus Christ.
He is the true God and eternal life.

1 JOHN 5:20

Lord, it seems like there is more encouragement to be fake than there is to be myself. Decisions about what is beautiful or worthy of attention are mostly made based on physical attractiveness or popularity. When I'm attracted toward changing who I am so I can be accepted, I have to hold tightly to Your love for me. It helps me remember that the real me matters more than the latest trend.

I won't always know if people like me for the right reasons—the heart reasons—but I do know one thing for certain: You are the true God, and the value I have as Your daughter is the real thing.

I'VE SEEN YOU

*Jesus answered, "I am the way and the truth
and the life. No one comes to the Father
except through me. If you really know me, you
will know my Father as well. From now on,
you do know him and have seen him."*

JOHN 14:6-7

Reading the Bible is a way to paint a great image in my mind of who You are and what You "look" like. Your Word provides me with a picture of who You are, what You're like, and how You love. Faith can be defined as belief in something unseen, yet my faith in You seems reinforced by what I feel and see in my daily life. I feel who You are when I experience the warmth of the sun, a reassuring hug from my mom, and the peace of prayer when I'm having a hard time. I see You when a friend smiles, when a challenge is resolved right before my eyes, and when I look at a cross.

Jesus, I love You. Thank You for showing me the love of my heavenly Father through the stories and promises of the Bible and through my daily encounters with everything You've given to me.

THE DECEPTION OF PERFECTION

*If we claim to be without sin, we deceive
ourselves and the truth is not in us.*

1 John 1:8

Lord, I have days that I have to talk myself up just to head out the door to school. There's so much pressure to maintain an image that sometimes I use half-truths to build myself up in front of friends. I've even told my parents that I wasn't to blame for something that happened because I didn't want them to think less of me. I can't keep pretending that I'm perfect or that I'm not struggling. The white lies of false cheerfulness start to separate me from my family, from You, and from my understanding of who the real me is anymore!

The deception of perfection is too much for me, and it keeps me from Your plan and purpose for my life. I want to get back to being real. Show me the way to honesty, integrity, and wholeness again, Lord.

Confidence

LET MY ACTIONS SPEAK

Speak up for those who cannot speak for themselves,
for the rights of all who are destitute.
Speak up and judge fairly;
defend the rights of the poor and needy.

PROVERBS 31:8-9

Lots of people are struggling with money these days. My family is extra careful with spending choices. Friends are worried about their families and their futures. I might be young, but I understand that people are hurting right now. They feel hopeless and scared.

Help me reach out to ease the burden of another. Who needs assistance? I can encourage a friend by being a good listener. Show me how to be helpful to my own family by being aware of what they are stressed about. And I want to be empathetic to anyone facing challenges. May I "speak up" through deeds, prayers, and choices to share Your abundant comfort and compassion with friends, family, and strangers.

LISTENING FOR YOUR VOICE

Can you raise your voice to the clouds
and cover yourself with a flood of water?
Do you send the lightning bolts on their way?
Do they report to you, "Here we are"?

JOB 38:34-35

Lord, my personal hurts take my breath away. I whisper to You in the silence of my room at night. The words I lift up are praises, because You are always here for me. I look for Your answers during this hard time. Even when my circumstances are tough, my soul is calmed as I lean into Your presence and listen for Your voice—the voice that the lightning and the waters pay attention to.

Lord, when You speak to my life, big changes can happen. I pray for guidance and a confident faith in my area of need. And I will use my voice to praise You for the transformation and hope You bring to my life with Your healing words.

LEADING BY EXAMPLE

Does not wisdom call out?
Does not understanding raise her voice?

PROVERBS 8:1

I try to be a good leader, Lord. I seek Your assistance when faced with decisions, and I pray about my every step. Please let my words be filled with Your wisdom. It can be intimidating to try to lead or inspire others. I want to influence my friends and others in good ways. If I study Your Word and keep talking to You, I know I will have a perspective and motivation more like Yours.

When I turn to You before speaking out, You give me understanding and guidance. My confidence is not in my abilities, but is in Your help at all times. In my desire to lead, Lord, let my life actions express Your message of love.

A SPIRIT OF STRENGTH

The Spirit God gave us does not make us timid,
but gives us power, love and self-discipline.

2 TIMOTHY 1:7

When I anticipate situations that make me nervous, I focus on the spirit of power You have given to me. I pray for fewer timid days as I learn to trust Your strength. Lord, give me a boldness I've never known. Let me step out having my security in You so I embrace the challenges and the joys with unwavering faith.

Life will be new and different as I make decisions, communicate, and walk forward in this power. I will practice self-discipline and express love through my actions so that You, Lord, may use this new confidence for good.

FEARLESS

Be strong and courageous, and do the work.
Do not be afraid or discouraged,
for the LORD God, my God, is with you.

1 CHRONICLES 28:20

I'm trying to be strong, Lord. I'm struggling lately because I've lost my way again. My thoughts are more about my fears than Your faithfulness and strength. Replace my negativity with courage and hope. If I rely only on my emotions, I slip backward or spiral downward. Please help me continue through the difficulties when I don't have the energy to keep going. Break my stubborn spirit so I learn to lean upon Your strength. It will be a relief to not be alone in this.

I pray to be willing to do the work of resting in Your truths. You are here with me always. When I lean into that promise…I am fearless!

CONFIDENCE TO ASK

*Ask and it will be given to you; seek and
you will find; knock and the door
will be opened to you. For everyone who
asks receives; the one who seeks finds;
and to the one who knocks, the door will be opened.*

MATTHEW 7:7-8

I've never been super comfortable asking for things from others. I'll tell my family about my wants, but when it comes to heart needs and hunger, I get quiet and reserved. I think about the possible rejection and ignore the desire in me to be known and seen by those in my life, including You. I consider other ways I could go about asking for assistance…the phone, an e-mail…a prayer…and they seem so much better suited to my personality than to boldly stand in front of the door and knock. I freeze up just thinking about standing there and asking for what I need face-to-face.

You require us to come to You…humbled, seeking, and thirsty. Lord, unfreeze me. Release my grip on excuses based in fear. I need not be afraid, because You will answer the door. But first…I must knock.

HEART TO HEART
ABOUT FAMILY

When you learn to depend on God to meet your needs, you can appreciate people even more because you do not expect them to meet every need you have. You are free to love people just as they are, regardless of what they can do for you.

Think about all the relationships in your life. Which ones most reflect God's loyalty to you? What is your family life like? Do you challenge your parents and their rules or decisions? Do you communicate with them and share about your day and your struggles? God is right there with you. If it feels like there is a wall between you and your family, ask God to help you find ways to connect with them.

When you feel let down by people...what need is not being met? (Examples: *They don't listen. They are not available enough and I feel lonely.*) How do you see God fulfilling that particular need?

Sometimes we demand too much of our friends or

family. List three times you have tried to "get your way" when you should have been willing to give in a little. How can you improve this behavior? What do you need from God to make that happen?

1.

2.

3.

Prayer Starter:

Dear God, okay…I have tried to do things my way as I relate to my family. It's hard to have everyone telling me what to do or how to be. As I strive to figure out who I am in You, I know I need to respect my parents and my family. They are helping me discover more about myself, if only I'll let them.

I pray for my family to draw closer together. Keep us physically healthy and also committed to paying attention to one another. May we learn to show one another Your compassion, even on the bad days.

I've noticed that I get the most upset with my family when they don't _____.

Help me turn to You in my need. And show me how to create more trust, kindness, joy, and faith in my family. Lord, lead me today. Guide me so that I can become closer to my family, especially to _____ (fill in a name or names). I pray for these specific areas of need in my family:

-

-

-

I lift up each member of my family today, one by one. As I speak their names to You, Lord, please give me a sense of their current needs or hurts. I trust You to be my source of inspiration and patience. Thanks, God. Amen.

Dancing

READY TO DANCE

There is a time for everything,
and a season for every activity under the heavens:
...a time to weep and a time to laugh,
a time to mourn and a time to dance.

ECCLESIASTES 3:1,4

I'm ready to laugh and dance, Lord. My joy is in You and from You. I have shed tears during hard times, and I've felt the sharp pain of loss. You and the people You bring to my life have been there to comfort me. But now I am ready to turn up the music of life and celebrate the many blessings.

I want to share my happiness with others too. How can I bring delight to my family? Which of my friends needs to be cheered up? Maybe a lot of my friends need a season of laughter and dancing. Show me the way to this new season, Lord. I want to embrace and embody the wonder of Your love.

THE HAPPY DANCE

Then young women will dance and be glad...
I will turn their mourning into gladness;
I will give them comfort and joy instead of sorrow.

JEREMIAH 31:13

Lord, I really need to quit complaining about my circumstances. How did I become so negative about myself and my life? I get bored. I blame my family if things aren't going well. I know that I take out my emotions on my friends. And I even get upset with You when I don't get my way. This isn't who I want to be.

I praise You for the many times You've released me from sadness. When I've needed a kind word, You remind me through the Bible and through special people that there's a lot of goodness to be recognized in my life. This makes me want to leap with joy. I feel free when I cast worries aside and then turn my eyes, heart, and mind toward You. Yes, today I will dance and be glad, because You have great things in store for me.

LEAP OF LOVE

You turned my wailing into dancing;
you removed my sackcloth and clothed me with joy,
that my heart may sing your praises and not be silent.

PSALM 30:11-12

I don't always feel heard. Sometimes, I might as well be speaking a foreign language to my family. At school, people talk when others are talking. There is rarely a moment when a full thought is expressed. It's hard to know when to try to share about my life and when to be quiet and let the moment pass. On the days when I want to give up and then give in to silence, You nudge me to speak to You and to share my heart. I'm so grateful that You listen and care. You understand me even when I cannot figure out my own feelings.

I know exactly how I'll break through my time of quiet desperation—I will twirl, jump, cheer, sing, rejoice, and shout out my praises to You today, Lord. You hear every whisper and every holler of my heart.

NEW MOVES

Again you will take up your timbrels
and go out to dance with the joyful.

JEREMIAH 31:4

I've been looking forward to change. I don't want life to be the same old thing over and over. But now that changes are taking place, I'm worried about the pieces of my self and my routine that must fall away to make room for new things.

Lord, be gentle with me as You mold me into a creation that serves You better. I know that Your vision for my life is worth the inconvenience and heartache of the growing pains. I want to celebrate this time of becoming more like You and more like the *me* You created me to be. I love how You are showing me new moves! Now it is time for me to dance with the joyful who lead a rich life of faith and trust.

Satisfaction

SATISFACTION

It is God who arms me with strength
and keeps my way secure.

PSALM 18:32

Heading toward adulthood has its benefits. When I give my days to You and seek Your direction, I notice simple and satisfying signs of growth. I'm strong enough to resist pressure to do something I believe is wrong. My words are kinder. My thoughts are more positive. And I'm quicker to help someone, often noticing a need they have that others might miss.

Even on the hard days, I am encouraged by Your strength. When I stand on the foundation of faith and look forward to all You have for me, the view is very satisfying.

WHEN I'M WEARY

I will refresh the weary and satisfy the faint.

JEREMIAH 31:25

I wish that downing an energy drink would transform me into someone vibrant and fabulous like the commercials show. I know that real renewal doesn't happen that way. And honestly, when I watch those pretend-happy people, it makes me more tired and a lot more frustrated with my boring routine.

I'm tired of being tired. I'm calling out to You for refreshment that buoys my spirits. God, I am thirsty for the kind of nourishment You offer my soul. If I become weary of trying to do good or of walking in Your will, infuse me with Your energy, strength, and passion. Direct me toward the people, decisions, words, and actions that lead to a fulfilling journey of faith. I want to be my best. Lord, lift me with Your Word and Your hope.

MORNING PRAYER

Satisfy us in the morning with your unfailing love,
that we may sing for joy and be glad all our days.

PSALM 90:14

God, mold my day with Your hands. Lead my heart with Your own. Give me the peace that comes with knowing, without a doubt, that I'm Your child and I'm loved unconditionally. I've had days when I believe my negative thoughts more than I believe Your Word and Your life-changing hope.

This morning, I need You. I want to start my day by expressing my gratitude to You for carrying me through good times and bad. Lord, You are so faithful. You give me everything I could possibly need to make it through this day, even if a few bumps and detours are a part of it. As the sun rises, You lift my spirit with Your lasting joy and gladness.

THE WOW OF VOWS

Then will I ever sing in praise of your name
and fulfill my vows day after day...
Truly my soul finds rest in God;
my salvation comes from him.

PSALMS 61:8–62:1

God, the day I made my commitment to follow You and make Your desires mine as well, I entered into a covenant, a sacred relationship that would impact my life forever. Today I felt as though I didn't fulfill my vows to be faithful and true. I walked away from a chance to speak up about You, and I felt bad about it all day. Yet, You are gentle and forgiving. No matter what I do, or don't do...You never withhold Your love. You never withhold Yourself.

My heart hums with praises because Your faithfulness shows me that I matter to the Creator of the world, to the Inventor of *me,* and to the One who always keeps His word.

HEART TO HEART
ABOUT BOYS

Just a guess…you and your friends spend time thinking and talking about boys. You notice guys more and you probably wonder whether they are noticing you. It's normal to develop a sense of anticipation and joy when you see or talk to a particular guy.

Because all of this thinking, daydreaming, smiling, and wondering is happening, it's also an important time to know yourself well, including how you are loved and valued as God's child. He wants the best for you. Seek guidance from His Word and from Him in prayer. Talk to your parents and trusted mentors as you explore feelings of fondness for a boy. Their wisdom will help you shape your convictions and dreams—both of which matter to your future self!

Is there a guy you like or one who likes you? When a boy becomes the object of your affection and the focus of your attention, stay grounded in your identity as a young woman of faith. This will help you maintain healthy

physical and emotional boundaries. Believe it or not...
the guidelines you set for yourself now and for your relationships with boys will lead to a life of greater joy. You'll
realize that confidence in God's purpose and promises for
you is the best gift you can give yourself.

Think of the traits a godly guy will have. Keep these in
mind as you talk to or make friends with boys. How will
a godly guy speak to you, about you, and about spiritual
realities? How will he treat others? In what ways will he
show respect? Know that you deserve the very best.

Trusting the ideals God has given you and holding on
to them is how you become a stronger, more empowered
you. The "future you" will be grateful.

Prayer Starter:

God, You see every interaction I have with people
and You know who I will meet along my life's
journey. Help me watch for those chances I have
to serve You through my actions and interactions
with others.

Help me understand what is best for me as I spend
more time with and around boys. Reveal to me how
to keep my behavior and conversations in line with
what I know to be Your hope for me. I want the
best now and later. I pray for strength to know what

I believe in and to stick with that, even when my emotions make me question my convictions.

I want to give You control over a couple of relationships in my life right now. Lord, help me specifically with the following areas:

-

-

-

I want my affection and attention to only go toward a boy who honors You and me. Help me maintain a healthy respect for myself, my body, and my heart, God. Amen.

What
Matters Most

WANT

Direct me in the path of your commands,
for there I find delight.

PSALM 119:35

My attention has been directed toward things I want. When my family and my home seem too close for comfort, I imagine what it'd be like to live at my friend's big, cool house. A clothing-store window downtown displays the perfect sweater at a ridiculously high price. Still, I've thought about how much better I'd feel in that top. And…as You know, I've spent a lot of time wondering if a particular guy likes me. I practice my smile and a casual "Hi" in case I see him.

I know these aren't bad aspects of life to think about, but when I dwell on things that are out of reach or out of my control, I lose sight of the good things that are here and now. Lord, reveal to me what my priorities and desires should be. May my wants line up with the delights that come straight from Your hand to my life.

IT'S NOT EASY

*To do what is right and just
is more acceptable to the LORD than sacrifice.*

PROVERBS 21:3

There's a good reason to make the right choice in a difficult situation: It pleases You. If it is difficult, so be it. If anyone gives me a hard time because of my commitment to do what is good and acceptable in Your sight, then at least they are noticing that there's a different way to live.

When I consider the approval, popularity, or even status I might be giving up by doing the right thing, remind me that I'm not losing a thing. Encourage me to gain momentum toward a life that pleases You and leads me toward my absolute best path.

PUTTING PRIDE ASIDE

He guides the humble in what is right
and teaches them his way.
All the ways of the LORD are loving and faithful
toward those who keep the demands of his covenant.

PSALM 25:9-10

Lord, give me a humble heart that's open to let You lead me. My pride gets in the way of my willingness to follow You. It's hard to let go of my ego, vanity, or stubbornness. All of these troubling traits flare up when I lack confidence. I guess I try to build myself up or talk others into seeing my value. I rarely end up with the results I aim for. My priorities get off track, and I lose my sense of purpose.

When I finally let my guard down and ask for my value and identity to be shaped by You, then I experience the love and trust You intend for me to live in. Help me put my pride aside so I learn Your way of light, humility, love, and promises.

THE GRACE OF GIVING

*Since you excel in everything—in faith, in speech,
in knowledge, in complete earnestness and in the
love we have kindled in you—see that you
also excel in this grace of giving.*

2 Corinthians 8:7

Thank You, God, for the good things and abilities You've given to me. As I increase my times of prayer and my commitment to what You want for me, I'm discovering more about myself and the gifts You've allowed into my life. When I do my best for You, Lord, I am succeeding. You don't tell me to be perfect, but You call me to excellence in my faith and my obedience. This makes me stronger, smarter, happier, and more eager than ever to be used by You in this world.

Whether good things come to me as opportunities, money resources, talents, or relationships, I pray that I will use them as my means to serve and inspire others. The grace of giving is one more way that You let me partner with You in great things.

Peace and
Freedom

WHAT CAN I DO?

*I urge...first of all, that petitions, prayers,
intercession and thanksgiving be made
for all people—for kings and all those in
authority, that we may live peaceful
and quiet lives in all godliness and holiness.*

1 Timothy 2:1-2

Lots of people are experiencing great struggles and hardships because of war, poverty, loss, and loneliness. It breaks my heart when I hear of those who are hurting in my town, state, country, and throughout the world. But what can I do, Lord?

I guess I'm doing the very thing I can do—pray! I don't have the power to change the flow of current events or turn heartache into blessing, but You do, Lord. I pray for the people in the situations I have on my heart. From world leaders to the children and families caught in the middle of conflict or injustice—may they feel Your leading and peace. Also, show me how to share Your peace and comfort with someone in my life this week.

I NEED YOUR PEACE

I will heal my people and will let them
enjoy abundant peace and security.

JEREMIAH 33:6

When I am feeling scattered and unable to concentrate,
    You are my peace.
When I'm worried about my family,
    You are my peace.
When I wish life were different,
    You are my peace.
When I'm crying and nobody but You sees my tears,
    You are my peace.
When I feel less important or less loved than others,
    You are my peace.
When I long for a friend who understands me,
    You are my peace.
When I wish I had a guy friend who appreciated my heart,
    You are my peace.
When I wonder what tomorrow will bring,
    You are my peace.
When I call out to You with doubts and longings,
    You, Lord, are my peace.

FREE TO RUN

I run in the path of your commands,
for you have broadened my understanding.

PSALM 119:32

When my parents tell me that kids do better with boundaries, it's easy to think they're only trying to justify their rules. Now that I'm a bit older and have faced more difficult choices, I understand why "commands" and teachings matter. I can't always trust my emotions in a situation. And my friends are great, but sometimes they make bad choices. When I turn in the direction You call me, and I run in the path of Your commands, I experience the freedom of moving forward with peace of mind and peace of spirit.

You set my heart free, Lord. You show me the way to go and ease my concerns and doubts. My small, insecure steps become bigger leaps because I have faith in Your ultimate love for me and my well-being. I'm free to run toward my purpose. Thank You, Lord!

EVEN WHEN I DON'T GET IT

Do not be anxious about anything,
but in every situation, by prayer and petition, with
thanksgiving, present your requests to God.
And the peace of God, which transcends all understanding,
will guard your hearts and your minds in Christ Jesus.

PHILIPPIANS 4:6-7

Here, with You, I let my guard down. A lot of people don't know what I'm really like. Some friends think I'm more confident than I am. Others think I'm not motivated in certain areas of life, when I actually do have goals and dreams in those directions. My parents sometimes see what they want to see, so I hold back from telling them about my worries and weaknesses.

Even if I don't understand all there is to know about Your ways, I do understand the peace that comes over me when I give myself over to You. It's not easy for me to trust people in my life. But Lord, when I sit before You, my troubled heart and mind are eased. Please show me how to share the real me with my family and friends. Give us opportunities to talk about the hard things so that we can experience Your peace and healing together.

TWENTY-FOUR HOURS

Do not worry about tomorrow,
for tomorrow will worry about itself.

MATTHEW 6:34

Here come the mental lists of things to do or possible obstacles to avoid. God, help me shift my focus and find things to be thankful for. I'm grateful for another chance to get things right, to do the right thing, and to love You with all of my being. I ask for Your peace right now so that I do not jump ahead to what *might* happen tomorrow, what difficulties *might* rise up for my family this year, or what small question *might* become a big challenge for me this week.

Your peace always brings me back to this moment. You don't ask me to predict my future. You don't make all troubles go away. You ask me to walk in faith through this single day with awareness of Your peace and Your promises. I dedicate the next 24 hours to You, Lord. May I live them without worry and with great joy.

Hunger and
Longing

WHAT'S THE MANNA?

He humbled you, causing you to hunger and then feeding you with manna, which neither you nor your ancestors had known, to teach you that man does not live on bread alone but on every word that comes from the mouth of the LORD.

DEUTERONOMY 8:3

When the Israelites were wandering in the desert and feared there would be no food and nourishment to sustain them, You sent manna from heaven. This strange substance was all they needed to keep following Your lead. Yet, they grumbled about the manna. You literally showered a miracle down on them, and all they could do was complain.

This story is a great reminder to me of the times I've asked You for something to satisfy my heart's hunger and then complained when I didn't like the answer, the hope, or the wisdom You provided. And how many times have I missed out on the manna You have showered down on me? Lord, help me see the blessings and the miracles You bring to my life in response to the needs of my body, mind, and spirit. And when my eyes are opened to these gifts, let me receive them with pure gratitude.

AT YOUR SERVICE

I was hungry and you gave me something to eat,
I was thirsty and you gave me something to drink,
I was a stranger and you invited me in,
I needed clothes and you clothed me,
I was sick and you looked after me,
I was in prison and you came to visit me.

MATTHEW 25:35-36

When I'm busy or self-focused, it becomes easy, or at least more convenient, to look past the needs of people around me. And when I do notice the heart cries, I become overwhelmed by the different ways that people are hungry, sick, tired, lonely, and imprisoned by circumstances. Renew my desire, God. I want to serve You by acknowledging the brokenness of people You bring into my life and stepping up to do something about it.

May I see You in the stranger who is hurting and the friend who needs to hear a word of encouragement. Give me a tender heart toward my own family, so that I serve them with Your unconditional love. Show me how to give without fear and without pride. I'm at Your service, Lord.

MISSION POSSIBLE

*Not that I have already obtained all this, or have
already arrived at my goal, but I press on to take hold
of that for which Christ Jesus took hold of me.*

PHILIPPIANS 3:12

Oh, how I want to be passionate about the purpose for
which You've claimed me and my life, Lord! I believe You
see me and my imperfections and still believe I can grow,
learn, and thrive as a woman of Yours and Your great
purpose. I get excited when I imagine a life of meaning
and big prospects, instead of life lived without the hope
You offer.

My life might have challenges, but I'm on a mission
possible because of Your love for me. I'm not perfect by
a long shot, but when I press on with a sense of meaning
and identity in You, I am more perfectly equipped to
accept this mission called life!

I'M HUNGRY

*Blessed are those who hunger and thirst for
righteousness, for they will be filled.*

MATTHEW 5:6

I'm hungry for many things: acceptance, love, purpose,
success, security. As I look at this list, I realize how little I
focus on my hunger for connection with You. It's difficult
to understand what that would look like in my life. Create
in me a desire to be true to You and to pursue more knowledge of You so that I can become a person of integrity,
who sees life from Your perspective.

The people in my life who are examples of godliness are
those who are respectable and honorable. I notice them
because they give You credit rather than seek out attention or praise for themselves. Let these models of holiness
spark my own thirst for a new way of living out my faith.

Decisions,
Decisions

WAITING, WONDERING

In the morning, LORD, you hear my voice;
in the morning I lay my requests before you
and wait expectantly.

PSALM 5:3

You know how impatient I become when I don't know which way to go, Lord. I don't even like to wait for web search results or for text responses. But the only way to grow in patience is to actually practice *being* patient. I'm going to work on this area of my faith. I lift up my requests to You today and wait with hope and expectation. You are so faithful. Guide me as I make big and small decisions. During the waiting hours, I will reflect on the many times You have provided me with instruction and inspiration.

I place my hope in You and will wait in wonder.

TRANSFORMED

Do not conform to the pattern of this world,
but be transformed by the renewing of your mind.
Then you will be able to test and approve what
God's will is—his good, pleasing and perfect will.

ROMANS 12:2

I've fallen in with the rhythm and pattern of the world. Even if it counters the pace and design of my own heart, it's easy to be rushed along with what is going on around me. Lord, keep me from conforming to the world's ideas and standards. Renew my heart and mind so that I understand Your will as I make decisions that impact my faith and my future. I want to think with thoughts that are pleasing to You. And I want to love with Your love.

The more I follow along in Your way, the more I will discover what it is to be changed from the inside out.

WHAT IS RIGHT?

I sought the LORD, and he answered me;
he delivered me from all my fears.

PSALM 34:4

God, which way do I go? I'm really torn about the choice I have to make. I'm unsure where to turn for direction, and the anxiety is building. My parents don't understand my dilemma. Friends have advice, but each one says something that seems to relate more to them than to me.

I guess I'm afraid to make a mistake; so here I stand, unable to move forward. Lord, I am coming to You today with a strong need for Your wisdom. I need confidence that comes from You as I step forward. Please deliver me from fear so I experience the fullness of a right, godly life. Show me how to open up to my parents so I can have their wisdom and support during this time of worry. You are with me every step of the way.

GOOD TOGETHER

Let us discern for ourselves what is right;
let us learn together what is good.

JOB 34:4

I have a pretty good understanding of what is right and what is wrong. But when I stand for goodness and godliness by myself, I feel uninspired and even lonely. I believe in myself and I believe in You. Each day I work to do the right thing, but I know I can't go this alone. Lead me to friends, mentors, and teachers who are learning what is good and striving to do right by You. I need the encouragement and community of others to step up my giving and my abundant living.

Direct me to the groups or gatherings where I can have fellowship and can gain momentum in my quest to do right. I want to be one of Your faithful children and be *among* Your faithful children.

Love

MY HEART

*May the Lord direct your hearts into God's
love and Christ's perseverance.*

2 Thessalonians 3:5

I love love. It feels so good to receive loving words and kind gestures from my family and friends. I'd like to experience that with a guy too. I know what love is because You've shown it to me through special people and through the acceptance that covers me when I pray. But when I'm lost in daily struggles, stress, and emotions, or when people I care about let me down, I start to doubt Your love and my worthiness to be loved.

When I'm angry at someone who has hurt me or I'm upset about a situation that leaves me feeling hopeless, help me turn my heart toward Your love. It covers me, protects me, embraces me, and upholds me. May I always measure what love is by the feeling I have in Your presence.

LOVE IS

Love is patient, love is kind. It does not envy, it does not boast, it is not proud. It does not dishonor others, it is not self-seeking, it is not easily angered, it keeps no record of wrongs. Love does not delight in evil but rejoices with the truth. It always protects, always trusts, always hopes, always perseveres.

1 Corinthians 13:4-7

The romantic love that fills the movie screen and my dreams can seem so indefinable and unattainable. That's why these verses matter a lot to me right now. I like to think about the guy who might love me someday. If I keep my head in the clouds of the world's vague understanding of love, I won't ever know what to look for. But You don't leave me hanging. You state it like it is; or rather, Your Word states it like love *should and can* be.

Thank You, Lord. I mean it. I'm going to memorize this verse and play it back to myself and my friends over and over. As we open our hearts to future love, may we never settle for a version that is fantasy rather than faith-filled. As I try to live out this definition of love, I pray that someday I would also receive a romantic love that follows this same recipe for the real thing.

COURAGEOUS LOVE

Be on your guard; stand firm in the
faith; be courageous; be strong.
Do everything in love.

1 Corinthians 16:13-14

"Do I really have to love *that* person?" It isn't easy to like, let alone love, certain people. I struggle to show love to my family sometimes. I have good friends who can make it hard to love them because of their bad choices, hurtful words, or times of being undependable. Show me how to love even when it is hard. Show me how to stand strong in my faith by doing everything with pure motives and godly compassion.

As I guard my heart from the harmfulness of sin, nudge me to keep my heart open to the courageous work of forgiveness, service, generosity, and unconditional love. Give me what it takes to stand firmly on the foundation of love even when it is the hardest thing to do.

LOVE ONE ANOTHER

Dear friends, let us love one another,
for love comes from God.

1 John 4:7

Love is a gift from You, and it is meant to be shared with others. I hold back from doing that because I'm afraid that my efforts won't be accepted. What if they reject me when I say, "I want to be here for you" or "You're really important to me"? What if they can't say it back to me or they act indifferent about it?

See how self-protective I can be? I laugh at how I over-think the details, but I hope that someday I can worry less and share more. God, help me become the girl who isn't afraid to extend Your love to others with confidence and without unnecessary expectations.

Inspiration

WHOLEHEARTEDLY

*Whatever you do, work at it with all your
heart, as working for the Lord,
not for human masters, since you know that you
will receive an inheritance from the Lord as a
reward. It is the Lord Christ you are serving.*

COLOSSIANS 3:23-24

It's exciting to watch the lives of people who live whole-heartedly for You. I want that kind of faith. Fill me with the energy and hope I need to live this way. When my days blur together and seem meaningless or my efforts don't result in immediate success, infuse me with renewed passion for the small and big actions. I can do homework with the intention to learn and to do a great job. I can reach out to a friend who needs to talk. I can help my parents by doing chores without being asked. I can serve You by waking up each day and recommitting my life to You.

Free me from all regret and forgive me for the times I fall short of what You want for me. I am eager to accept the inheritance of a life inspired by You and the remark-able dreams You place on my heart.

ALL OF ME

Jesus replied: "Love the Lord your God with all your heart and with all your soul and with all your mind." This is the first and greatest commandment.

MATTHEW 22:37-38

This is my vow for this week, this month: I will give You all my heart and all my soul and all my mind. I'll consider it an official experiment of living out my relationship with You the way You intended. May I see each day as a new opportunity to show You my love and my commitment. I pray for insight and encouragement so that I would be inspired to press on in this way of living. This could be a radical change for me and my relationships—am I ready? I think so!

Give me a heart that wants to know Your heart. I'm excited to actively and attentively follow Jesus' greatest commandment. This renewed commitment will be what carries me through the days when I'm tempted to settle for less.

MEDITATING ON YOUR WONDER

They speak of the glorious splendor of your majesty—
and I will meditate on your wonderful works.
They tell of the power of your awesome works—
and I will proclaim your great deeds.

PSALM 145:5-6

Let me notice Your wonderful works! Give me eyes to take in each and every miracle that I encounter as I go about my daily routine. I know there are many examples of Your goodness, love, and power.

I've never been able to spend much time in silence. My mind fills up with ideas, worries, and doubts. These distracting thoughts crowd out my joy and belief. Help me be patient and still. Restore to me the delight and wonder that I felt as a young child first discovering the cool sting of snow, the sweet surprise of a pear, and the great comfort of a hug from my dad. These simple pleasures speak of Your splendor and direct my wandering thoughts toward the path of pure inspiration.

PASSION AND PURPOSE

This is how we know that we love the children of God:
by loving God and carrying out his commands. In
fact, this is love for God: to keep his commands.

1 John 5:2-3

In the world I'm exposed to, the concept of passion is often attached to romantic love or sex. God, as a believer, I know that passion is also about following You and the purpose You designed me for with every ounce of energy and commitment I have. Ignite in me a passion to live as Your child and to love Your children, including people at school I don't always agree with and my family when we aren't connecting enough.

I'll know that I'm following Your passion when I let go of my pride and my limited expectations and start to live out Your commands. Passion is about love—a fantastic love for life, for my unique reason for existing, and for my Savior!

Purity

PROTECT ME

How I long for your precepts!
In your righteousness preserve my life.

Psalm 119:40

I've made a mess of things, and there is no one to blame except my stubborn self. I wish I could wake up some morning and know everything! I want to get how the world works, how boys think, how my heart works, and how I can be true to Your calling in my life as I sift through the confusion surrounding love, like, and everything in between.

I need Your support and assurances now more than ever. Keep me from being flirtatious or untrue to myself around guys. I let my impulses get the best of me when I'd rather let the best of me (You!) take over the situation. Protect me through the rise and fall of feelings I have for guys so that I preserve my purity and pure intentions.

THE PEACE OF PURITY

The fruit of that righteousness will be peace;
its effect will be quietness and confidence forever.

ISAIAH 32:17

The girls I know who lose their power, identity, and purity to guys seem to lose their confidence along the way too. I've watched this happen to girls who have or had the same beliefs that I hold onto. I've experienced it myself in certain ways and am just reclaiming my peace in You and Your righteousness. I'm so grateful that I'm growing in faith and that You are there to show me love and forgiveness.

Lord, keep me from sacrificing my righteousness and my confidence. I want to receive my power, identity, and peace from You alone.

SWEET

Know also that wisdom is like honey for you:
If you find it, there is a future hope for you,
and your hope will not be cut off.

PROVERBS 24:14

I think the commitment to stay pure and to resist sexual temptation can seem old-fashioned or simple, but it's a lot more complicated than when my parents and other adults were young. They try to understand how hard it is, but I don't know that they do. "Sweet sixteen" and beyond requires confidence, faith, commitment, and trust. I suppose it always did. Either way, You see what my friends and I have to counter in our culture to remain true to our values. I believe we all need Your help.

I'm grateful that my spiritual, physical, and emotional health and wholeness matters to You, Lord. I hold on to this truth to help me resist sexual activity and temptations. Your loving plans fill me with the hope of a sweet future. That's worth waiting for.

IT WON'T BE TAKEN AWAY

"Martha, Martha," the Lord answered,
"you are worried and upset about
many things, but few things are needed—
or indeed only one. Mary has chosen what is better,
and it will not be taken away from her."

LUKE 10:41-42

Without my intention or permission, I feel like much of my purity has been taken away. I've experienced or been influenced by false promises and negativity. Exposure to temptations and opportunities to do the wrong thing arise all the time. I ask for forgiveness for the times I fall short of Your best for me.

I have placed importance on the wrong things. And now I'm afraid that my wholeness is lost because I shifted my focus from the one thing that mattered—You. Your peace covers me and confirms what I know deep down to be true: My devotion to You and Your love for me will never be taken away.

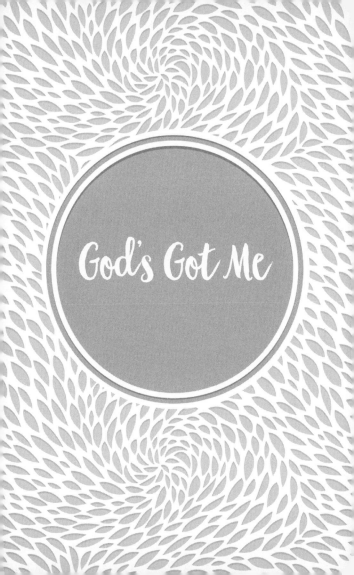

God's Got Me

WHAT'S THE WORRY?

Who of you by worrying can add a single hour to your life?
Since you cannot do this very little thing,
why do you worry about the rest?

LUKE 12:25-26

If I had a dollar for every hour I've spent worrying about my life, I'd be able to go on a very wonderful shopping spree. It isn't that I'm unhappy with my life—I feel blessed in many ways. But the worry is clearly there, and my mind latches onto the concerns and anxieties and doesn't let go of them.

Who am I to think I can change anything yesterday or today by worrying? Teach me to relax enough to lean into You for answers, peace, and comfort. I don't want to spend one more single hour serving the god of worry when the God of life and hope is my Lord.

BECAUSE OF HOPE

You will be secure, because there is hope;
you will look about you and take your rest in safety.

JOB 11:18

I'm so lucky to have faith, Lord. As friends and I face similar struggles and doubts, I realize how my trust in You offers me the security and hope some of them don't have. We all are looking around us for an answer to our immediate problem, whatever that might be: a bad hair day, a breakup, a fight with a parent, a health problem, or a day when our hearts and minds keep asking, "What *is* the meaning of life?"

But when I hear Your voice and read Your Word, I look around me only long enough to look to You. I don't rely on false truths or shallow answers from the world. I have the peace, safety, and comfort of hope in You. You hold me and my life in Your hand. I'm forever grateful.

COVER ME

*If that is how God clothes the grass of the field, which
is here today and tomorrow is thrown into the fire, will
he not much more clothe you—you of little faith?*

MATTHEW 6:30

Lord, I want a balanced perspective about what really matters. If I have clothes to wear and have food and shelter, what more could I want, right? Well, the desire and concern for what is in my closet still creeps into my days. I can't seem to let go of this preoccupation, even though I want to be someone who doesn't get caught up in all of that.

Give me a mature grasp of what's important to You and what should be of importance to me. You promise to clothe me, to provide for me, to care for the details of my journey. When I take on extra worry about such material things, I am not placing faith in Your promises. Cover me, Lord. I want to be clothed in godly perspective and adorned with attributes of faith.

THE GOOD LIFE

*Our people must learn to devote
themselves to doing what is good,
in order to provide for urgent needs
and not live unproductive lives.*

TITUS 3:14

If today unfolds like a typical day, I will have labeled numerous things as "good" before dinnertime: a friend's new bag, a teacher's lesson, a book I've read. But I wonder what I'll create, inspire, say, or do that is good in Your eyes. I pray for opportunities to generate goodness that affects people positively. I pray that my productivity would move me forward in what You desire for me.

I'm discovering more about my unique traits, abilities, and desires. When I give them to You as an offering, they can be used for good in this world and to bring You praise. They also become my way to be productive and to provide for the needs of myself and others. Each day I walk in this truth is a day during which I can bring goodness to light and appreciate goodness when it crosses my path.

Something
New

WE GO WAY BACK

From birth I have relied on you;
you brought me forth from my mother's womb.
I will ever praise you.

PSALM 71:6

Nobody knows me like You do. You brought me into this world and now You bring me through this life. I praise You today for every stage of my growth. Thank You for giving me life and for showing me why living with You as my love and guide will lead me to purpose and meaning. I'm already experiencing that as I try to be a young woman who lives trusting You.

You are the One who was with me at my beginning and will be the One to embrace me at the end of my days. Thank You for being there and giving me encouragement and strength every day in between. Because You are with me, the start of something new feels exciting and hopeful.

MY FIRST CONVERSATION

I rise before dawn and cry for help;
I have put my hope in your word.
My eyes stay open through the watches of the night,
that I may meditate on your promises.

Psalm 119:147-148

To start my day off right, I come to You, Lord. You hear each and every word I speak. You listen closely to catch the timid prayers my heart lifts up. This day is unlike any other. Help me remember this when the alarm goes off and I start to think about the day's needs, or before I start complaining about how this morning feels so much like yesterday that I don't want to leave the bed.

The hope You give to me is the beginning of my possibilities, my dreams, my future. I will keep watch with attention to detail so that I don't miss out on situations, conversation, and connections that reveal how You lead and love me. Let me put my trust in Your promises and make this a day like no other!

A PURE HEART

Create in me a pure heart, O God, and
renew a steadfast spirit within me.

PSALM 51:10

I need a spiritual do-over. I give my heart away too easily to things of the world. I try too hard to please others, and I become like the person they want me to be. I love this verse so much, Lord. It gives me hope for my life today and for my future. Create in me a pure heart. Lord, mend its tears, heal the wounds, and bathe it in Your mercy.

God, renew a steadfast spirit in me. Show me how to stay true to what You want for me. I know how precious I am to You. I don't want to waste my heart on trivial pursuits. I recommit my life and love to You today because You make all things new.

THE START OF SMART

*The fear of the LORD is the beginning of wisdom,
and knowledge of the Holy One is understanding.*

PROVERBS 9:10

You know my secret. I mask my fear and intimidation with fake confidence and overly brave actions. I'm a lot of talk and show on days when I'd rather curl up and stay quiet or disappear. Why am I intimidated by so many opportunities and people? You give me a brain and mind to absorb information, to process ideas, and to make decisions—so why do I feel clueless most of the time?

I pray to ask for Your strength, confidence, and guidance in more circumstances. May I ground myself in Your wisdom as my start to becoming smart in Your ways. I look forward to understanding the people and situations in my world as a result of knowing You more intimately.

NEW LIFE

*We were...buried with him through baptism
into death in order that, just as Christ was
raised from the dead through the glory of
the Father, we too may live a new life.*

ROMANS 6:4

When I gave my heart to You, Lord, my new life began.
You freed me of past sins and gave me a way to turn over
my brokenness to the power of Your resurrection. On the
days when I fall back into the ways of old, show me how
to turn things around. Set me in motion toward bright
potential as I seek out Your presence and priorities.

God, show me how to live out this new conviction
and purpose. I want to share my renewed commitment
to You with others and never hold back my gratitude for a
Creator who allows new beginnings to happen every day.

HEART TO HEART
ABOUT UNIQUENESS

Have you ever held back from expressing your beliefs or opinion because you were unsure how it would be received or what people would think of you? Next time you pause before expressing yourself, think about this: Being *you* in any given situation is also about expressing God's creation. He made you unique and filled you with ideas and dreams and abilities. Sure, we all need information, guidance, and lots of prayer…but those are ways to enhance the special being in each of us.

Think about what makes you special. Don't be shy… make it a daily practice to thank God for one aspect of your unique self and life. And while you are at it…encourage another person about their unique self or something they tried or accomplished. They might need a reminder about how great they are. Recognizing the special traits and gifts of others is a great way to honor and acknowledge the living God.

List five ways you can express the true you this week.

1.

2.

3.

4.

5.

Prayer Starter:

God, reveal to me my specialness. Help me preserve my integrity and build my confidence in You so I am able to nurture the gifts and dreams planted in my heart. Direct me to a deeper understanding of who I am in You. I want to be a reflection of You each day. Help me recognize the special gifts I have so I don't miss out on using them and growing them. These are the areas of strength I recognize in myself right now:

-

-

-

This week, I pray for Your help in a particular area. While I develop my strengths, I also want to build strength in these areas of weakness:

-

-

-

Thank You for loving me…all of me. Amen.

Reaching Out

INTEREST IN OTHERS

*Do nothing out of selfish ambition or vain
conceit. Rather, in humility value others above
yourselves, not looking to your own interests
but each of you to the interests of the others.*

PHILIPPIANS 2:3-4

For a time I tried to stay super busy so everyone would think my life was great and full. I kept up appearances because I never wanted anyone to know that I actually felt empty and alone. For a while it worked, but then my false world fell apart because there was no life in my life.

Give me eyes to look beyond myself so that I notice the needs of others. Fill me with compassion and empathy. Lead me to become a caring presence for my friends, a listening ear to someone I don't often notice, and a helpful hand to a person in need. Let my interest in others replace my self-focus, Lord. When I reach out to others, I don't have to pretend life is full...because it *is* full.

PASS THE SALT

Be wise in the way you act toward outsiders;
make the most of every opportunity.
Let your conversation be always full
of grace, seasoned with salt,
so that you may know how to answer everyone.

Colossians 4:5-6

I love to sprinkle salt on my popcorn, French fries, and green beans. You ask me to add a similar spark and flavor to my communication with others by sprinkling the conversation with Your love and grace. I need to remember this when bitter words or sarcasm are about to leap off my tongue.

Give me tenderness and affection toward people I encounter. Remind me to smile and greet waiters, baristas, and the sweet old man who walks his dog in our neighborhood. Keep me from indifference or self-protection so that I notice someone at school who needs a dose of kindness and generosity. Let me be one who is willing to pass the spark of salt and the flavor of faith on to others.

SOMETHING BORROWED

If anyone forces you to go one mile,
go with them two miles.
Give to the one who asks you, and do
not turn away from the one
who wants to borrow from you.

MATTHEW 5:41-42

Giving without strings attached goes against the culture. Getting and acquiring are important. Achieving is expected. Receiving is desired. But giving is often overlooked in a person's first response to a situation or to a person. I want to be someone who gives unselfishly. If a teacher asks me step up my concentration in class, help me say yes with respect. When someone asks to borrow something, let me say yes without bartering to get something in return. If a friend asks for a favor, let me say yes without complaint. And help me honor my parents by saying yes to their authority without them having to ask me.

I draw mercy and forgiveness from Your endless supply, Lord. Why waste another day hoarding such gifts? Today, I will come to You and ask to borrow the patience, kindness, and love I need to go that extra mile.

ONE IN SPIRIT

If you have any encouragement from being
united with Christ, if any comfort from his
love, if any common sharing in the Spirit,
if any tenderness and compassion, then make my
joy complete by being like-minded, having the
same love, being one in spirit and of one mind.

PHILIPPIANS 2:1-2

I want to be connected to the body of Christ with a strong thread of tenderness and love. Church offers a community that helps me discover more about Your love and about myself. I do feel cared for when Christian adults and teachers take time to get to know me. When they take time to listen and show respect for my ideas and thoughts, I sense I am valued even though I'm young.

Fellowship is a gift from You, and I should embrace it fully. God, give me the strength and the opportunity to invite a friend to church. It is a source of encouragement and inspiration. As I grow in my understanding of what it means to be one in spirit with other believers, may I also look to give the gift of belonging to someone else.

Faithfulness

OUT-IN-THE-OPEN DEVOTION

*Now devote your heart and soul to
seeking the LORD your God.*

1 CHRONICLES 22:19

When I played hide-and-seek, I liked to stay hidden in my secret place until I heard the kids who were already safe or caught laughing and yelling. That's when I'd feel more lonely than victorious, so I'd rush into the open and make a run for home.

I don't want to be good at hiding from You. I become lonely when I distance myself from Your way of life. I want to be a girl who seeks You and Your guidance and doesn't pull back when You call my name. I wonder where I'll discover You today. When I do see things of You, I'll put my heart of devotion out in the open so everyone can see that You are my home!

THE FAITHFUL ONE

*Know therefore that the LORD your God
is God; he is the faithful God,
keeping his covenant of love to a thousand generations of
those who love him and keep his commandments.*

DEUTERONOMY 7:9

I want people in my life to be truthful and faithful, but sadly, they disappoint me. When I become discouraged by their imperfection and my own, I concentrate on Your faithfulness. You shaped the heavens and the earth, and even though I'm just a speck in the universe, You love me unconditionally. You provide for my needs. You listen to me night and day. And You shepherd me toward safety and comfort.

When I feel like a blip on the timeline of eternity, I can embrace my significance as a believer in the faithful One who has kept His covenant of love to believers of every generation…including me. I love You.

ONE OR THE OTHER

*No one can serve two masters. Either you will
hate the one and love the other, or you will
be devoted to the one and despise the other.
You cannot serve both God and money.*

LUKE 16:13

A minister once said that you can tell a lot about a person's priorities by looking at how they spend their money. If their records show that their income goes to new clothes, takeout food, movies, and lottery tickets, then they might be letting money and the material world become their masters. They might be forgetting all about serving God and others.

I don't have much money or other resources, but help me find ways to serve You with what I do have—time and willingness. I can read to children at the library, serve at church, and volunteer for charities I believe in. I want my faithfulness to be evident as I make choices and start good habits of devotion today.

TOO MANY MAYBES

All you need to say is simply "Yes" or "No";
anything beyond this comes from the evil one.

MATTHEW 5:37

Lord, I need Your strength to stick to my convictions…
and my answers! I haven't followed through with some of
my responsibilities. In fact, I'm reluctant to make com-
mitments because of my history of breaking them. Sometimes I just lose interest in finishing what I've started.
Other times, my trust in You isn't strong enough to stand
behind my decisions. I don't want to be a "maybe" person.
I want to be a girl whose word counts.

When a path veers away from Your plan for me, let my
voice and actions be used to say "No." But when there is
an opportunity to walk forward in the way You lead me,
then let my "Yes" be unwavering. Guide me to be a young
woman of integrity.

Hope

RESTING IN YOU

Yes, my soul, find rest in God;
my hope comes from him.

PSALM 62:5

A situation in my life has become a big burden. I've let it build and now it's a huge, dark cloud hovering over me. I can't seem to let go of it or get out from under it. People have failed me. I've even let myself down. You are my refuge and hope, Lord. When will I trust You completely?

Sometimes I lie in bed and wonder what my later years will be like. Will I find happiness? Will I have hard times? Alone times? Love? Adventure? All of the above? I'm always the girl with questions, aren't I? At least I understand that You are the answer, no matter what tomorrow brings. For this time, please give me a right and truthful perspective on my problem. Clear away the dark cloud so the light of Your help can shine on the right next step.

AS THE DAY IS LONG

Show me your ways, Lord,
teach me your paths.
Guide me in your truth and teach me,
for you are God my Savior,
and my hope is in you all day long.

Psalm 25:4-5

I like to go outside at night and look up at the stars. I love the vastness of the night sky. My heart immediately calls out to You, "Show me the way, God. Show me the next step." I find that I'm much more desperate for Your guidance than I realize during the day. I think I try to stay busy so I don't have to call out for help. But I know You want me to seek Your teachings and truths. So, show me, Lord. Show me.

Lord, I pray for my hope to multiply and to fill the space of my heart like the stars fill the sky. Maybe then I will learn to place my hope in You all day long.

TIRED OF WAITING

I wait for the Lord, my whole being waits,
and in his word I put my hope.

Psalm 130:5

Yes, I'm young. But everything is young compared to You, right? Even though I haven't experienced as much as my parents or teachers, I've still had to wait and wait for guidance. I struggle to be patient, but it's important that I place my hope in You. Expressing those words isn't just a casual thing for me. I believe You are the keeper of my dreams and my future.

This time in my life is so important, and the work You're doing in my life is incredibly important. So I will place my hope in You forever. I will wait, pray, and listen. And once I've done that, I will do it again.

PROTECT ME

We wait in hope for the LORD;
he is our help and our shield.

PSALM 33:20

Without a doubt, I will need help today. I need protection from my bad habits, from bad influences, and from the negative thoughts I have on a regular basis. There are people in my life who are supportive and encouraging. I'm not in this alone. But I don't always trust my judgment, and I need the shield of Your protection.

I'll give You my troubles today in exchange for Your strength. I know that isn't a fair trade. That's the incredible beauty of the gift You give me, the gift of You. Life isn't easy for teenagers, and I need all the help and hope I can get.

Contentment

OPEN HEART

Restore to me the joy of your salvation
and grant me a willing spirit, to sustain me.

PSALM 51:12

I'm excited to have a clean slate today, Lord. Grant me a spirit that welcomes the people, conversations, situations, and even the struggles that arise. I don't want my focus to be on possible failings or fallen pride. As soon as I do that, I miss out on the joy of being open to how You are leading me.

If my perspective has become jaded, forgive me. Lead me back to the joy and hope of my salvation. Show me how to release my burdens so I will have open arms and an open heart ready to receive the joy You intend for this faith journey.

ENOUGH

Godliness with contentment is great gain.
For we brought nothing into the world,
and we can take nothing out of it.
But if we have food and clothing,
we will be content with that.

1 Timothy 6:6-8

There is too much stuff in my closet, on my shelves, in my locker, and on my mind. Most of the clutter is made up of things—from clothes to worries—that don't fit my life anymore. These unnecessary bits and pieces of physical and emotional baggage distract me from godliness. The weight of them keeps me from the lightness of contentment.

God, I need Your discernment so that I can make better choices about what fills up my personal and spiritual space. Temper my desire to want everything I see. Keep me from wanting what I know I can't have. Satisfaction won't come with stuff; it will only come when I discover the life You intended for me. It's under here somewhere! And I know it will be more than enough for my every need.

JOY

You make known to me the path of life;
you will fill me with joy in your presence,
with eternal pleasures at your right hand.

PSALM 16:11

My friend and I got lost the other day. We weren't trying to get to a physical location, but we were trying to navigate our way through a difference of opinion. It was rocky at first, but then we found footing in our common ground. We can actually laugh about it now. And I feel closer to her because we made it past a small bump in the road together.

This experience reminded me how my relationship with You grows deeper and stronger when I trust Your strength to get me through a difficult time and back onto solid ground. In Your perfect way, I draw closer to joy and contentment when I draw closer to Your heart. May I learn to rush into Your presence with great expectations for a friendship that lasts an eternity.

A WILLING HEART

Submit to God and be at peace with him;
in this way prosperity will come to you.

JOB 22:21

Submission isn't easy for me, God. You know how stubborn I become when You or my parents ask me to do something I don't want to do. I'm sorry that I greet Your requests with resistance instead of cooperation. I have always equated submission to giving in or giving up. Yet, when I see others humbly and graciously follow Your guidance, I admire their strength. And I recognize their peace as deep and real.

Give me the wisdom and courage to give myself over to You fully. I want to experience the abundance and goodness that flows through an open, willing heart.

Promises

RIGHT-SIDE UP

*You know with all your heart and soul
that not one of all the good promises the
Lord your God gave you has failed.*

Joshua 23:14

The emotional roller coaster I've been on has turned my sense of direction upside down. I actually thought I could place faith in my strength alone. How could I forget Your faithfulness to me and to my spiritual walk? God, Your promises have sustained me and my family. Each day, even a hard one, provides evidence of Your provision and care.

I know with all of my heart and soul that You've never failed me. Your Word is good. Your promises are good. Your intention for my life is good. I pray that these truths will keep me and my faith upright when life throws me for a loop.

CLUELESS AND COMMITTED

As you do not know the path of the wind,
or how the body is formed in a mother's womb,
so you cannot understand the work of
God, the Maker of all things.

ECCLESIASTES 11:5

I'll confess to You that I'm clueless. Often I pretend to know how the world works and who I am in it. I guess I want my parents and friends to think I'm in control. But You see through my brave words and bold actions to my uncertain heart. At first, it scared me to be so vulnerable. But You reassured me that the many miracles, wonders, and daily happenings that baffle me are all in Your control.

Admitting what I don't know gives me peace. Now I can fully embrace what I do know: You are the Maker of all things and You care about me. I might be clueless about many things, but I'm certain of my commitment to the One who intimately knows me, my heart, and my future. Today, I'll rest in the not knowing, and I will praise You, the all-knowing lover of my soul.

PLANS AND PROMISES

*"I know the plans I have for you," declares
the* LORD, *"plans to prosper you
and not to harm you, plans to give you hope
and a future. Then you will call on me
and come and pray to me, and I will listen to you."*

JEREMIAH 29:11-12

Am I walking in the right direction, Lord? I'm giving this situation over to You and Your wisdom, God. Help me let go of choices, wants, or beliefs that don't fit in with Your best for me and my future. Reveal to me what is good, right, and true. I don't want to waste my time following detours when there is a plan made and shaped just for me.

Each day that I move forward in what You desire for me, I'm unwrapping the gift of Your promises for my life. Help me discover ways to share this gift with others. I want people in my world to understand the wonder and power of Your faithfulness.

CAN YOU HEAR ME?

You, Lord, are forgiving and good,
abounding in love to all who call to you.

PSALM 86:5

Lord, hear my prayers today. I have much to bring to You. My mind and heart are filled with concerns and praises. As soon as I opened my eyes this morning, I was aware of how much I needed to bring before You. I kept my distance for a while because of feelings of shame. My stubbornness caused me to feel unloved and unwanted.

But You are my Redeemer and my Savior. I need not return to old patterns of thinking and behavior, because Your promises give me a new direction. I can come to You anytime because You love me, You forgive me, and You accept me. I have so much to tell You.

HOLD ON TO HOPE

Let us hold unswervingly to the hope we
profess, for he who promised is faithful.

HEBREWS 10:23

Life offers many choices. And with each one, there is a risk. But my hope in You, Lord, is never a risk. You're my one true thing. My constant. Now if I could just live that out with the conviction I feel right in this moment. God, help me through times of doubt. Don't let me speak of Your hope one day and then run scared as soon as something or someone challenges my belief.

Your promises never hold me back; instead, they give me hope to hold on to as my dreams take flight.

HEART TO HEART
ABOUT YOUR FUTURE

Isn't it amazing how many times people ask you at this age, "What do you want to do with your life?" Like you should have it all figured out! A typical girl probably imagines herself in at least five different careers. Anything from a veterinarian to an actress…these can all seem valid at this point. But truthfully, God is already planting seeds for your future life. In the times when you feel like very little is happening, He is likely planting some seeds. If this is the time you are facing now…prepare to harvest good things.

When you face the times of waiting, praying, and watching for God's lead, don't worry about being behind or off track. He is working in your life. In fact, He's doing great things right now. Maybe you're ignoring them. Maybe you're taking credit for them. Or maybe you're just beginning to realize the wonders He is doing in and through your experiences and seasons of waiting and growth. Your future is a full one…rich with God's provision and direction.

List four things you think God is doing in your life right now:

1.

2.

3.

4.

Think about how you see your future self. How is your faith today a part of that plan for tomorrow?

Prayer Starter:

God, You hold my today and my future in Your hand. You have a purpose for me, yet sometimes I forget to ask You about the life You have planned for me—including what the rest of today should look like. Strengthen me as I move forward in what You want me to do. Help me release these particular worries to Your care so I can walk by faith toward my future:

-
-
-

I want to be an influence for good today…right where I am. Thank You for being by my side, for leading the way, for knowing my future, for preparing me now for any trials, and for the great things to come. I love that our conversation will continue for the rest of my life. You are my comfort, my guide, and the keeper of my heart, God. Thank You for loving me. Amen.

About the Author

Hope Lyda is an author whose devotionals, novels, and prayer books, including the popular *One-Minute Prayers® for Women* and *Life as a Prayer*, have sold over one million copies. Her inspirational books reflect her desire to embrace and deepen faith while journeying to God's mystery and wonder.

Hope has worked in publishing for more than 20 years, writing and coming alongside other writers to help them shape their heart messages and mine their experiences to connect with others. As a trained spiritual director, she loves to help others enter God's presence and pay attention to their authentic, unique life and purpose. Her greatest joy is to find ways to extend these invitations through the written word and writing exercises.

Learn more at www.hopelyda.com

Follow on Instagram at @hopelydawrites

MORE FAVORITE READS FROM HOPE LYDA

One-Minute Prayers® for Comfort and Healing

One-Minute Prayers® for Men

One-Minute Prayers® for Men gift editions
(coauthored with Nick Harrison)

One-Minute Prayers® for Moms

One-Minute Prayers® for Wives

One-Minute Prayers® for Women (all editions)

One-Minute Prayers® to Start Your Day

One-Minute Prayers® to Unwind a Worried Mind

One Minute with Jesus for Women

Life as a Prayer

The Gift of Small Blessings

The Gift of Small Comforts

This Little Light of Mine

AVAILABLE ONLY AS E-BOOK

One-Minute Prayers® from the Bible

Altar Call (fiction)

Hip to Be Square (fiction)

Life, Libby, and the Pursuit of Happiness (fiction)